# THE TOP THREE
# SCHOLARSHIP
# HACKING
## SECRET$

### Unique, Easy and Proven Strategies
### No One Else is Talking About

**JEANNIE SCHULMAN**

ISBN: 978-1-4834-8063-3 (sc)
ISBN: 978-1-4834-8062-6 (e)

Lulu Publishing Services rev. date: 2/8/2018

# DEDICATION

*A big shout out to my amazing family! I am so blessed to have each of you in my life. You bring me joy, purpose, and adventure. I love you... Marc, Joshua, Caley, Jenna, Krista, Kayla, Scott, Christina, Casey, and Hailey.*

*A special thank you to my husband, Marc, who is always so encouraging and supportive. You're the best! Thank you so much for your unconditional love and for helping make this book a reality.*

*To the members of our Secret Scholarship Club... you all are AMAZING! I KNOW you will each go far in life, achieve your dreams and make a huge impact on the world. Krista, Kayla, Katie, Savannah, Jackie, Merryn, Reece, and Andrew... I DEDICATE THIS BOOK TO YOU! It's been an honor to help you with the scholarship process. You are all outstanding individuals, and I'm so proud of you.*

*THANK YOU to everyone who reads this book and puts its principles into practice. You have a great future ahead of you. The world will be a better place because of YOU!*

# ACKNOWLEDGMENT

I would like to acknowledge and thank my friend, Peter Ainley, who provided invaluable guidance and expertise right when I needed it as I wrote this book. Peter, you helped take this project to the next level. Thank you! His coaching services can be found at www.soaringwitheaglesint.com.

I would also like to thank Kevin Drapal for all his technical support. Kevin, you're a ROCK STAR!

Thank you to Stephanie, Teri and the team at Lulu Publishing for all your hard work and dedication to this book project. You were all wonderful to work with throughout the entire process.

Thank you to Kim Cormier for my author photo. She believes photography is a way of looking at the world and creating images in a creative and unique way that people will treasure for a lifetime. Her Website is: http://kimcormierphotography.zenfolio.com/.

# CONTENTS

# TESTIMONIALS

*Jeannie's Top Three Scholarship Hacking Secrets helped me earn thousands of dollars of scholarship money, and now I'm on the fast track to graduate college with money that was given to me!*                                    Cassidi O.

*Winning the Kohl's scholarship when I was 12 years old was an exciting achievement for me! Because I started Secret #1 when I was really young, it enabled me to win this prestigious scholarship. They are holding the scholarship money for me until I go to college in a couple years. Anyone can win scholarships… it doesn't matter how old you are!*                                    Kayla M.

*As the pressures of my senior year built and the season of applying for scholarships and colleges arrived, I was very nervous that I hadn't done enough to get into a good college. I felt like I was behind the rest of my classmates. Thanks to Jeannie and her book about how to earn scholarship money, I learned how to write winning essays and format my résumé in a way that made it stand out to the judges. I also learned how I could use Secret #1 to set me apart from the competition. I was so relieved to learn that even the small things I've done in high school would give me a good chance at winning money. I'm currently a senior and have been applying for scholarships. So far, I've won $100,000 in scholarships, I'm interviewing for different full-ride scholarships, and I'm in the running to win more.*                                    Krista M.

*Mrs. Schulman has given me valuable advice for winning thousands of dollars of scholarship money and also for succeeding in future jobs. She's given me step-by-step instructions about how to do Secret #2 which will help my scholarship applications stand out. She also personally revised and edited my poorly written résumé into a stellar résumé. She truly has a gift, and I am so honored that she was willing to share her trade secrets with me.*                                    Jackie J.

*Mrs. Schulman taught me how to write short but effective essays that pack a massive amount of detail. She's helped me to specifically address each essay to speak the language the scholarship judges were looking for. The skills I've learned through The Top Three Scholarship Hacking Secrets and her Résumé and Essay Writing Program are not only beneficial for college essays, but also for public speaking, interviews, and other writing/speaking assignments.*     Reece L.

*Jeannie Schulman is an incredible woman who has given me many opportunities to implement Secret #1 and Secret #2 into my life. She's provided encouragement, love, and support in helping me achieve my goals. Jeannie has sacrificially taken time to help me with my homework, write my scholarship résumé, and have heart-to-heart conversations. She has effortlessly been selfless to me for the many years I've spent with her. I cannot thank her enough for how she's impacted my life. She's helped shape me into the woman I am today, as well as guided me and given me the tools to build a successful life.*     Katie B.

*After only two sessions with Mrs. Schulman I was able to perfect my résumé, come up with ideas that set me apart from the crowd, and write essays that are not only good for college but for the rest of my education. I feel more confident about my chances of getting scholarships and have felt much less stressed after meeting with her.*     Merryn D.

*I've learned so much about the top scholarship hacking secrets, thanks to Mrs. Schulman! She taught me how to do Secret #2 which was something I always wanted to do but never did. Because of these three amazing secrets, I now have the confidence I need to win scholarship money. I now know I'll be able to go to the college of my choice without the stress of money.*     Savannah T.

*It's not an exaggeration to say I would not be where I am today without the scholarships I received. Going to college has easily been the most life-changing experience I've ever had. I'm eternally grateful for the guidance, encouragement, and scholarship-writing tips Jeannie Schulman (aka Mom) taught me.* Jenna M.

# FOREWORD

My name is Jenna, and I am currently a junior at Colorado State University. It's not an exaggeration to say I would not be where I am today without the scholarships I received. Going to college has easily been the most life-changing experience I've ever had. I'm eternally grateful for the guidance, encouragement, and scholarship-writing tips Jeannie Schulman (aka Mom) taught me.

I never thought I'd be able to say that I not only have my entire four years of higher education already paid for, but because of all of the scholarships I was able to earn, I can also say that I'm currently being *paid* to go to college!

These scholarships made it possible for me to focus more on my academics because I don't need to worry about working long hours to pay for my education. I've also had the time to meet new people and get involved in meaningful experiences and groups that I genuinely care about.

In fact, next semester I will be attending Semester at Sea, where I will spend my semester voyaging across the world: taking classes on a ship and exploring 11 different countries! Despite the high cost of attendance, I still get the chance to participate in this once-in-a-lifetime opportunity because of the scholarships I received years ago. They cover the cost of the voyage, allowing me to fulfill my dream of studying abroad. Because of the extra expense of Semester at Sea, I've applied for other scholarships to help pay for extra expenses like international flights and visas. You can continue applying for scholarships even while you are in college!

College has been an incredible experience that has made me learn and grow more than I ever have before. I can confidently say I would not have been able to do half the things I've done so far without the scholarships.

If you truly want to make the most of your education and college experience, I urge you to follow Mrs. Jeannie's recommendations. You will be turned down for scholarships and you may feel as though applying for scholarships is a full-time job, but don't be discouraged! I remember how frustrating it was to fill out application after application, but I will forever be thankful to my past self for working hard and not giving up after a few rejections.

Everyone has something unique to bring to the table, so harness that and apply for as many scholarships as you can. There are a world of opportunities out there waiting for you as long as you are willing to reach for them!

# PREFACE

Excitement filled the air as graduation approached. Senior pranks were being planned, graduation announcements were being ordered, and students were trying to ignore their senioritis. Some of the seniors were excited about venturing out into the world, while others didn't have a clue as to what they were going to do *for the rest of their lives*.

Cassidi was a bit uncertain about *what* she wanted to study in college. However, she knew exactly *where* she wanted to go. Her two options were a local college in the town where she grew up, and a great college that everyone wanted to attend in a nearby trendy city. Cassidi had her heart set on going to the college alive with action, but it was more expensive than the local college. Like so many students her age, the thought of paying the extra money per year was daunting. She would have to maintain a job throughout college, and her parents would have to work extra hours just to afford the tuition. I remember talking to Cassidi about where she was planning to go to college after she graduated, and she explained her dilemma. My heart went out to her, because she was like a daughter to me, and I wanted the best for her.

Cassidi is like millions of other students who have a dream of attending a certain college but cannot afford the ridiculous cost. Cassidi was fortunate to win enough scholarship money to at least level the financial playing field. She is attending the college of her choice, but she still has to hold down a job to remain there.

We found ourselves in a similar situation as Cassidi. We had some unexpected medical expenses that resulted in our not having enough money for our daughter, Jenna, to attend a more expensive college. As you will read about in this book, we discovered a few secrets that gave Jenna the competitive advantage, helped her win over $100,000 in scholarships and grants, and enabled her to go to the college of her dreams. *Right now, she is going to college without spending a dime of her own money.*

Because I believe everyone should have the opportunity to go to college if they want to, I'm revealing the top three secrets we used to help all my children win scholarship money for college. I believe there is enough money to go around, and if you apply the secrets found in this book, you will have a chance at winning a piece of the billions of dollars of scholarship money given out every year.

Now I'm guessing for a lot of you, this is probably not your first shot at the whole "scholarship thing." Please know that if you've failed at winning scholarship money in the past, or if you're not even sure where to start, it's not your fault. There's a lot of information out there, and it can be confusing. Many times that "information overload" keeps you from success. It's okay.

If you've been concerned in the past that you just can't succeed, I want to put those fears to rest. You can do this. You just need the right person to explain it to you.

The college establishment wants you to think that college legitimately costs as much as it does, and you just need to come up with every penny to pay for it. I'm here to tell you, that's a misconception.

If you've ever thought the establishment just wants to squeeze every penny out of you that they can, you're probably right. They don't make money from *not* charging you an arm and a leg. They want you to think that in order to make money in the future, you need a good education. And the only way to get a good education is to hand over all your hard-earned money. Does this make sense? The difference with me is that I actually care about your success and truly want to see you living the life of your dreams.

So that's what I'm here for. I know you have a dream to get a great education, pursue your passions, and make an impact on the world. I want to show you how to make that dream a reality.

My goal for this book is to help two types of people. For those who are beginners, you'll learn how to get started on the often-daunting task of applying for scholarships without feeling stressed out, overworked or bored. For more experienced people, you'll learn how to outsmart, outlast and outmaneuver your competition.

Let's take a look at two things that are true for both the beginner and the more experienced person...

1.  The only way to win thousands of dollars of scholarship money is by getting ahead of the competition.
2.  The only way to get ahead of the competition is by learning the three unique strategies we used to win tens of thousands of dollars in scholarship money.

Traditionally, colleges send you a bill for housing, food, books and tuition, and you cough up whatever they charge you. That's not easy for the average person to do. You end up taking on huge loans that you promise to pay back later, when you may or may not have a job. You just accept this as normal and think this is the only way you can get the education you desire. This is the worst way to pay for college because it straps you to a lifetime of interest and debt. You end up paying more than you originally signed up for, and your future self ends up regretting this decision.

Applying for scholarships and using the techniques we used to win tens of thousands of dollars in scholarship money is the smarter solution. You spend a little bit of time on the front end, which saves you years of working on the back end.

This method didn't just work for my children. My husband and I helped some of their friends apply for scholarships, perfect their essays and write professional looking résumés, and they won scholarships as well.

In this book, we're going to cover three things...

1. How to win thousands of dollars in scholarship money by implementing one of the top three secrets
2. How to know where to start and what to do
3. How to apply for scholarships without feeling stressed out, overworked or bored

I wrote this book for all the students who want to achieve their dreams and attend the college of their choice. I wrote it for all the parents who are stressed out about the rising cost of college tuition and weren't able to save enough money to help their children out. And I wrote it for all those who know there is a smarter way to pay for college than to be strapped to a lifetime of debt.

I'm here to tell you… there's hope! You have the answers in your hands. If you diligently apply the secrets within these pages, you *will* outsmart, outlast and outmaneuver your competition.

# CHAPTER 1

## RISING FROM THE ASHES

### 🖋 GOING FROM $0 TO $100,000+

Six months after Hurricane Katrina swept through the city of New Orleans in 2005, leaving devastation and desperation in its wake, our family packed up and moved to the heart of it all. Like so many other families, we were struggling to make it. Everyone was feeling the symptoms that ultimately led to the housing bubble that burst in 2008. We had four small children whose little lives and futures were in our hands. Struggling to put food on the table, the thought of providing a college education for them was something that seemed like a mirage in the desert... a hopeful wish that was always out of reach.

*Have you ever felt that way?*

Construction work was abundant in New Orleans so, as in the gold rush days of the 1800s in California, we journeyed to the place that held promises of hope. Hope for a better future. Hope to get out of the rat race. And hope that the lives of our children would be better than our own.

When we arrived, we were shaken to the core by what we saw. So many people lost everything. The only things left standing were the foundations their houses once stood upon. There were houses *on top of* cars *#howdidthatevenhappen?* - and clothes were hanging from branches of trees. In an effort to clean up the city in the months that followed, mountains of trash were piled in the streets.

I remember seeing broken cribs, moldy rolls of carpet and damaged trophies. Seeing the trophies amidst the rubble was a sobering sight. I was gripped by the realization that, in a moment, all the "trophies" we hold close to our heart may be carelessly tossed into a heap of trash. It was then that I realized the only things that can withstand the "hurricanes" of life are things that have true lasting value... your character, your faith and the people you love.

As you read through this practical guide on how to build a strong future for yourself or for your children by winning scholarship money, remember that this isn't *only* about winning money to create the future of your dreams. It is much more than that.

Throughout the process, you will win in ways money can't buy. You will become a stronger person who is able to contribute to society in altruistic ways. You will meet new people and build relationships that are the key to unlocking doors you would not otherwise be able to open on your own. And most importantly, you will be left proudly holding a trophy that cannot be destroyed.

# CHAPTER 2
## THE STRATEGY

🗞 I'M JUST A NORMAL PERSON. HOW CAN I WIN AGAINST OTHER SUPERHUMANS?

*I Am A Scholarship Hacker!*

🗞 WHICH ONE ARE YOU?

There are two types of people who say, "I'm just a normal person..." and then ask, "How can I win against other *Superhumans*?" The first type of person is the one who actually *is* Superhuman. Do you know someone like this? They have over a 4.0 GPA, they are the President of every organization, and their hair is always perfect. However, they don't *feel* Superhuman because they don't recognize their superpowers, they doubt their abilities, or they compare themselves with other people.

The second type of person is the Clark Kent type. They get average grades, they'd rather be playing video games, and they just put a cap on whenever their hair gets messy. They *are* normal but they haven't put their cape on and tapped into the power within.

*Who do you know like this? Which one are you?*

In *The Top Three Scholarship Hacking Secrets,* you will learn the three secrets to rise above the Superhumans. Whether you're a Superhuman or a Clark Kent, you will learn the top three easy, unique and proven strategies to winning thousands of dollars of scholarship money for college.

## ALARMING STATS

Did you know that 44 million Americans owe over $1.4 trillion in student loan debt? In fact, the average Class of 2016 graduate has $37,172 in student loan debt (https://studentloanhero.com/student-loan-debt-statistics/). *Wouldn't you love to go to the college of your dreams without spending a dime of your own money?*

Can you imagine what it would be like to go to your high school graduation, walk up on stage and hear them list scholarship after scholarship you won?

And wouldn't it be awesome to walk across the stage at your college graduation knowing you have a degree in your hand and a clean slate on which to build a strong future?

That would be pretty awesome, right?

When my children were at the age when they needed to start preparing for college, I realized we didn't have any money saved for them... and neither did they! When I was in college, I paid for my bachelor's degree through scholarships, grants and by working. Consequently, I just assumed that's what other people did as well. I must have pounded that idea into my children's heads when they were young, because I remember walking into their bedroom one time and overhearing my daughter's Barbie dolls "talking" about earning scholarships to go to college!

Scholarships were always at the forefront of our minds as a way to pay for college but as novices, we really didn't know what we were doing or where to start. When it came time to start thinking about college, time was short and I knew we needed to come up with a solution... *fast!* So we sat down, **looked at our past** and thought about how we could **optimize it for the benefit** of winning scholarship money.

## ✐ OPTIMIZING YOUR PAST: DOING VOLUNTEER WORK

Our past has been a mix of both struggle and service. Ever since the kids were little, we've been involved with our local church and have participated in all sorts of outreach activities. We did volunteer projects as a family, and as a result, the kids learned to be generous and think of other people. We helped in the church nursery, delivered plates of goodies to people in the community and wrapped Christmas presents for people at the mall for free *#givingyouideas*. Even though we didn't start the scholarship application process until the kids were in high school, we actually got started when they were young.

When we were in New Orleans, we had a plethora of opportunities to help people. People were really struggling. Their lives were absolutely torn apart. The church even seemed helpless and dark. Simple things for people, like doing laundry, were difficult. I remember going to the laundry mat and waiting like a hungry vulture (like everyone else) to get a washing machine. People were desperate; so desperate that my laundry basket even came up missing one time!

Even though our living conditions were actually physically as bad as they were for the people who endured Katrina, that didn't stop us from doing what we could to help others. We filled Easter baskets with treats and delivered them to neighborhoods near the church. We filled Christmas mugs with hot chocolate and candy canes and delivered them to people living in FEMA trailers. Here's a picture of Kayla ready to deliver the goodies. *#nineyearslatershewonthekohlsscholarship!*

At the one-year anniversary of Katrina, we delivered 3,500 Hurricane Preparedness kits (with flashlights, batteries, hurricane preparedness lists, and Christian literature) to people in the community. Our church back home donated the money to do this, and "work teams" who came to our church in New Orleans helped package and deliver them. Wanting to participate, my kids strapped on their roller skates and skated from house to house hanging the kits on peoples' doors.

Here is a picture of the kids delivering supplies to families living in FEMA trailers.

These stories serve as an example of how you can be a strong force in your own community. It's no secret that volunteering and doing community service is one of the main ways you can earn scholarship money *#staytunedforthetopthreesecrets*. Don't underestimate the power of serving others. As you give to others, it will be returned to you.

## MAKING IT WORK

Everything we did for people was out of love and service. However, when we began to think about applying for scholarships, I realized we could **take what we did in the past and strategically plan to do more**

**of it.** At that moment, we made a conscious decision to plan out all our volunteer work for the year and start accumulating and tracking hours. Volunteering in your school and community is one of the main things scholarship judges look for when considering who wins scholarships. It shows that you care and that you are a leader. In the following chapters, you will see how we took volunteering (which many high achieving students do) to the next level.

## OPTIMIZING YOUR PAST: OVERCOMING OBSTACLES

One of the other ways we optimized our past was to take a tragedy and turn it into something that could inspire other people and win the hearts of the scholarship judges. You're probably aware that this is essential when writing scholarship essays.

Here is an excerpt from an essay written by Jenna, one of our daughters. It talks about a life event she overcame, how it impacted her and how it helped her grow into the person she is today *#jennawon$100,000+*. Jenna wrote this essay as a freshman in college because she was applying for more scholarships. *Did you know you could do that?* Some of the scholarships offered by colleges are reserved for those in a certain field or of a certain grade. Remember to research and apply for scholarships even after you get to college.

Scholarship judges like to hear colorful and descriptive essay *stories*, not just a list of accomplishments. The story doesn't have to be tragic because, often times, great people are those with a healthy and solid background. However, one question that is frequently asked by scholarship committees is, *"What obstacle have you overcome and how did it impact your life?"*

Thinking about your own life, the struggles you've faced both internally and externally, and how you rose above those obstacles will be helpful as you answer that question. Reading other peoples' essays will give you ideas on how to write your own.

## JENNA'S STORY

*"When I was eight years old, my family and I moved to New Orleans to help rebuild the city after Hurricane Katrina took its devastating toll on the community. Although we had to live in undesirable (and often unsafe) conditions with another family from India, our mission was to serve those who had lost so much. I remember taking gifts to people living in FEMA trailers, helping rebuild a church for the deaf, and roller skating from door to door in the New Orleans heat to deliver Hurricane Preparedness kits during the one-year anniversary of Katrina.*

*After being in New Orleans a couple years, we loaded up our meager possessions to head back home.*

*It was Christmas Eve 2008 and we had just gotten on the interstate. A big semi-truck whizzed past us, and the force of the vehicle caused our trailer to start swerving. We rolled several times, just missing a concrete bridge support, and we landed in a snowy field. This was the third auto accident I was in within a four-month period… and the beginning of my life taking a drastic turn.*

*I sustained injuries to my back and neck and have been in different types of physical therapy treatment since 2008. A year after the rollover, I was in another accident where our vehicle hit a bull on an open country road. And months after that, a car turned in front of us and caused me to be in yet another auto accident.*

*Because of these unusual circumstances and the pain that ensued, I wasn't able to play sports or engage in the same type of physical activities that my peers did. Instead, I poured myself into volunteer work through school and in my community. While in high school, I co-founded a philanthropic organization, called IMPACT, which is still in existence today. IMPACT has served the community and world in so many unique ways such as raising money to buy toys, clothes, school supplies, and hygiene items to be sent to impoverished children overseas, as well as sewing dresses for girls in third world countries.*

*I've spent almost half my life receiving treatment for my back and neck injuries. I understand discouragement and pain, but I also understand perseverance and the power of rising above my situation. "I've learned that perseverance is not a long race; it is many short races one after the other." - Walter Elliot*

*I split most of my time between college and my job as a bank teller. I'm always striving to keep a high GPA, do well in the Honors Community, Presidential Leadership program and in Alpha Phi Omega. I also strive to uphold the standards as an Anschutz Scholar and participate in community service events. Too many people, when faced with obstacles and discouragements, crumble under the pressure. Thomas Edison said it so well... "Many of life's failures are people who did not realize how close they were to success when they gave up."*

*My past experiences, although difficult, have made me into the woman I am today. Through them, I discovered who I was and what I am made of. I dug deep and found strength, fortitude, and perseverance. As a result of my past, I am better able to empathize with and encourage others who have mental or physical challenges."*

If we could somehow give Jenna her youthful body back in lieu of all the scholarship monies she won, we would. But we can't. She took the deck of cards she was dealt and played her hand well. She won by not becoming bitter, not giving up, and not letting her past dictate her future. This is what scholarship judges want to see.

They want to see someone who will drum up the strength within and do something good for themselves and for others. They want to see someone who will take the challenges life throws at them and rise above them. It's not about what happened to you in your past; it's about how you respond to it and who you become because of it.

## ✏ A WORD ON THE SCHOLARSHIP ESSAY

*When you write your scholarship essay, paint a picture with your words and show this to the scholarship judges. Bring them to the place you experienced your obstacle, help them to feel what you felt, and inspire them with how you responded.* Everyone, even the people who are reading your essay, can benefit from your personal story.

Please remember not to compare your story with others. Just because you don't have a better "tragedy" than someone else doesn't mean you won't win. Take a good look at your own personal past, and write down all the things you can build on when you write your essay. **Your life and your experiences are unique and should be honored.**

Two of the most common ways to win scholarships are by doing community service work and by writing a good essay. You're smart. You already knew that, right? In the next chapter, I will tell you about how our daughter, Jenna, is going to the college of her dreams without spending a dime of her own money. And in the chapter after that, *I will reveal the top three scholarship hacking secrets you can use to become a Superhuman! Get ready!*

## A WORD ON THE SCHOLARSHIP ESSAY

# CHAPTER 3
## $100,000+ AND COUNTING!

### 🪶 HOW CAN I WIN THAT MUCH MONEY?

I have four biological children, and all of them have won scholarships already. We are getting ready to begin applying for more scholarships for the fourth. Jenna will complete college debt-free, which includes studying abroad for a semester. Her contribution toward her college education was a result of the community service she did before she graduated from high school, as well as her stellar grades. She was involved in a variety of organizations where she held different positions at school, including Key Club. Key Club is a great service organization in which to participate. Tuition for the college she attends is over $27,000 per year, and the cost of studying abroad is in excess of $39,000 for one semester.

She's been able to pay for this completely through scholarships and grants. The total amount she's been awarded is over $100,000, and she's not even finished! One of the scholarships she won is only awarded to the top five incoming freshmen at her college each year. That scholarship alone was worth $36,000. When she graduates from college, she will be well on her way to building a solid future without being enslaved to tens of thousands of dollars of debt in student loans.

When Jenna was a freshman in college, all of her scholarship money went to pay for tuition, books, fees, housing in the dorm as well as a meal plan at the cafeteria. When she moved off campus into her own apartment, the scholarship money automatically paid for tuition, books, and fees. Because there was a significant amount of money left over, the college deposited it directly into her checking account. Did you know that's how it works? Jenna budgeted the remaining portion of scholarship money to pay for her apartment rent, utilities, food, gas for her car and miscellaneous expenses. When you are awarded with grants and scholarships and live off-campus, it's your responsibility to make those dollars stretch and use them wisely.

Just to clarify, scholarships are monies awarded to you from colleges and community service organizations based on academic or other achievements. Grants are monies awarded to you by your state or local government, corporation, foundation or trust based on your grades, income or because you are attending college in your own state. The Pell Grant is a federal grant and is based on your family's income. You can receive the Pell Grant after you apply for the FAFSA. Neither grants nor scholarships need to be paid back.

If you do not receive enough scholarships or grants, you have the option to get a parent loan or student loan to pay for college. Loans need to be paid back after you graduate from college. Focus your attention on implementing one or more of the top three scholarship hacking secrets, presenting your résumé and essays in a dynamic way, and applying for a lot of scholarships. Think about what your ultimate goal is (win $100,000, win $200,000) and strive for that. All of the smaller scholarships add up quickly, and you'll be glad you did the work to receive them.

When my children were in high school, they spent their free time participating in groups, playing sports, and working. The things they did to earn scholarship money were fun! They made new friends, brightened peoples' days, and they were filled with the joy that comes from serving others. You really can't beat "getting paid to go to college" by doing things like that! Jenna literally earned her way through college by having a blast (serving others) in high school.

When my youngest daughter was 12 years old, she won the Kohl's Regional Scholarship. The *KOHL'S* scholarship *#justanotherreasonilovetoshopthere!* I will explain in detail how she won later.

I read about one student who applied for over 300 scholarships! That's exhausting just thinking about it. Jenna applied for less than 20. I believe her high success rate of winning so many of the scholarships was because she strategically applied *just one* of the three secrets in this book.

I'm excited about passing the valuable lessons and secrets I've learned on to you, so you can take your success to awesome heights. Your journey begins now!

*Are you ready to find out what the top three scholarship hacking secrets are?*

# CHAPTER 4
## THE TOP THREE SCHOLARSHIP HACKING SECRETS

**WHAT ARE THE SECRETS THAT WILL SET ME APART FROM OTHER PEOPLE AND HELP ME WIN MONEY, MONEY, MONEY?**

With the competitive nature of high schools and colleges these days, you must do something *EXTRA* to set yourself apart from other high achieving students. In addition to having good grades and being involved in your school and community, the best way to accomplish this is to do at least one of the following:

*SECRET #1:* **BECOME THE FOUNDER OF A COMMUNITY SERVICE ORGANIZATION**

*SECRET #2:* **BECOME A BUSINESS OWNER**

*SECRET #3:* **BECOME A PROJECT MANAGER**

You might be surprised to discover you are already doing one or more of these things to some extent. In the following chapters, I will cover each of the secrets in depth and tell you why they will set you apart from your peers and give you a step-by-step guide to implement them. It's all about looking at what you're doing now and taking it to the next level.

I personally believe this is why my children have consistently won thousands of dollars of scholarship money. Collectively, they did #1. My son did #2. And the other two daughters are working on doing #3. You do not have to do all three of them. **One is enough** if you dedicate enough time and effort to it.

The high school my children attend is very competitive. All three of my daughters have achieved beyond a 4.0 GPA. When Jenna was a senior, she had a weighted GPA of 4.3. HOWEVER... none of my children are the top-performing students in their class. Their GPAs are about one one-hundredth of a point away from the next student in line. It's crazy! **With competition like that, they had to do something unique to stand out from the crowd.**

That being said, please understand if you are an average student, YOU CAN STILL DO ONE OF THE TOP THREE SECRETS AND WIN SCHOLARSHIP MONEY. It's more about showing you are a LEADER than about having a 4.0 GPA.

I will go over each of the three secrets to success in depth in the following chapters. Be thinking about which of the three strategies would be the best fit for you.

## BECOME THE FOUNDER OF A COMMUNITY SERVICE ORGANIZATION

The first of the top three scholarship hacking secrets is to become the Founder of a community service organization. Take a look at what you've done in the past or what you're currently doing and create a group that encompasses those things. Many of your peers are involved in school clubs such as Key Club, right? Maybe even you are. Would you agree that they are also doing volunteer work in the community? You may be as well. So how do you stand out from the crowd? Here's the secret: **take the initiative to form your own community service organization and invite other people to be a part of it.** Do you see how this is different from what your "competitors" are doing? Do you see how it takes you from being just a volunteer to a leader? Your peers may be part of a club, but you will be the founder and leader of a club. If you're already doing community service work outside of a school club, create your own organization and let all that extra community service work fall under the group you created. That's how you take what you're doing now to the next level.

The crazy thing is... you can do the exact same volunteer work as one of your peers, but you will gain the edge simply because all your community service work is under the organization you created. This is how you differentiate yourself from other "Superhumans." Does that make sense? Doing this will not only develop your leadership skills, but it will show the scholarship judges you are the type of person who goes the extra mile. There are certain skills needed to run an organization or project, such as dedication, organization, and passion. You will show the scholarship judges you possess these highly favored qualities.

My four children co-founded a student-led community service organization called *IMPACT*. It's basically them and their friends doing a variety of fun and meaningful projects in the community – whatever they come up with! They created a special Facebook page to document all the projects they complete. It's an easy way to keep track of the projects via pictures and videos. When they apply for scholarships, they include the Facebook link on their scholarship résumé and application. It's a great way for the scholarship judges to see all they've done.

**Here are some of their cool projects, which you can do as well if you create your own group:**

- Volunteered at FOCO soup kitchen (and even got Cutco #cutcorocks! to donate $600 worth of knives to the soup kitchen - simply by emailing and asking them!)
- Performed door-to-door fundraising to purchase toys, school supplies and hygiene items for impoverished children overseas. Some people asked for a donation receipt, so we made our own, printed them up and had them available to give to people who requested one.
- Filled shoeboxes with toys, school supplies, and hygiene items to send to impoverished children overseas annually (through *Operation Christmas Child*)

- Worked at the *Operation Christmas Child* Distribution Center annually (There are different centers in major cities where you can volunteer)
- Bought nutritional products such as protein bars and protein shakes and sent them to US military troops (http://www.nutritioncoach.us/)
- Performed *Random Acts of Christmas Kindness*
- Baked cookies for the police station and the fire department (The fire department said the police station *always* gets the goodies! LOL!)
- Made Valentine cards for seniors (through *Meals-on-Wheels*)
- Collected teddy bears and donated them to a local hospital (inspired by *Harper's Hugs*)
- Sewed dresses for impoverished girls overseas (through *Dress-A-Girl Around the World*)
- Volunteered for community gardening and donated the food to a local food bank
- Volunteered regularly at a *Hearts & Horses Therapeutic Riding Center*
- Collected blankets and towels and donated them to the *Humane Society*
- Collected toys and art supplies and donated them to the *Boys & Girls Club*
- Volunteered at *Adaptive Adventures*
- Donated winter clothes to a local Refugee Center
- Raised money for a charity by performing in a concert with several bands

## HOW DO I CREATE MY OWN COMMUNITY SERVICE ORGANIZATION?

Creating a community service organization and becoming the Founder of the organization is easy. You can have a core group of people who run it (President, Vice President, Secretary, Treasurer) and then invite a variety of different people to participate in the activities you plan.

If you want to create an organization with a friend, group of friends or family members, they can become Co-Founders of the organization. They would become the group that makes all the decisions and runs the organization. When you have service projects planned, you can then invite other people to participate. You can also invite people to be a part of your group, and they can attend meetings and help plan activities.

*IMPACT* started in our living room. As the kids got older each year, they took on higher positions in the organization. They have all had the opportunity to have the prestigious role as President. **It looks really impressive to put that you were a Founder/President of an organization on your scholarship résumé.**

Just to give you an idea how cool it is, here's what the community service heading of my daughter's résumé looks like. Listed are a few of the service activities she helped lead. Please note the detail she put into each bulleted point. The more specific you can be regarding your activities and involvement, the better. This alone will set you far ahead of your competition.

**COMMUNITY SERVICE PROJECTS**
IMPACT CO-Founder & President    facebook.com/wemakeanimpact
*City, State*                                                       *2013-present*

- **Co-founded and led a community service organization called IMPACT** whose mission is to make a positive impact in our community and world by doing a variety of projects for people in need

- **IMPACT has collectively volunteered over 1,000 hours with 22 volunteers**

- **Raised $390** through door-to-door fundraising to purchase toys, clothes, school supplies, and hygiene items for poverty-stricken children in third-world countries; Filled up to 14 shoeboxes with gifts to be shipped to other countries each year; Each project took about 10 hours

- **Worked on the assembly line at Denver Distribution Center** and processed hundreds of boxes of toys, clothes, school supplies and hygiene items for *Operation Christmas Child*; Project done annually; 6-8 hour time commitment; The IMPACT group collectively volunteered over 675 hours

- **Sewed 10 dresses for girls in third-world countries**; Spent 50+ hours sewing dresses; Taught 3 other people how to sew dresses; Group has sewn about 20 dresses and completed 100 hours of sewing *(2015-present)*

Underneath the heading is a bulleted list of what she's done in *IMPACT* and what the group has done as a whole. Krista included her individual hours for each project, as well as the number of collective *group* hours. Because she was the Co-Founder and President of this group, she was able to say that *IMPACT* sewed dresses for impoverished girls in third-world countries for 100 hours, as well as to say she personally sewed 10 dresses.

One of her peers may have done a similar project but just listed it under "Community Service Projects" along with other projects he/she did.

That person's résumé heading and bulleted points may look like this:

**COMMUNITY SERVICE PROJECTS**
*City, State*                                                    *2013-present*

- Volunteered at Operation Christmas Child
- Volunteered at Dress-A-Girl Around the World
- Volunteered at a Soup Kitchen

The difference here is that Krista created a group, got other people involved and led the activities. And for that, she earned the title of President. If you're able to do the same, you will stand out among your peers. Which heading looks better to you, and which one do you think would catch the attention of the scholarship judges? Which set of bulleted points looks more impressive? Even though it takes extra time and effort to tally up the hours, results and additional information, it is one of the most important aspects of writing a great résumé.

**If you are already doing community service projects (outside of school clubs), take it to the next level and create a community service organization.** It only takes a few extra steps and a little more involvement.

If you discover a project you enjoy, you can do it annually or multiple times, or you can do a project once. It's really important to keep track of the number of hours you serve, the number of dollars you spend, and the number of items you donate. The scholarship committees like to see NUMBERS! If you give them SPECIFICS, you will stand out among your peers.

You can create a Microsoft Excel spreadsheet or a Microsoft Word document to keep track of all the projects you do, the number of hours spent, etc. You can also make notes in your phone and keep track of it that way until you have time to organize it in a better way, like in a spreadsheet. Another great way to keep track of your volunteer hours is to use the *Track It Forward* app. You can keep track of your individual volunteer hours or the hours of each member in your group.

To brand your community service organization, you can create a logo for your group, make t-shirts and other cool items (like pens and stationery) and hold meetings. Vistaprint.com is a great site to buy inexpensive items to promote your organization.

Honor the work done in your group by awarding certificates of achievement such as Most Hours Served, Highest Contribution, Most Valuable Member, or Outstanding Contribution. You can include these awards under the "Award" section of your scholarship résumé or on applications. You can create awards by using the "Certificate" template in Word.

If you're really ambitious, you can do the work to create a 501(c)(3) Nonprofit Organization. You can create a Nonprofit Organization by going to your state's Website and following the steps they give. A list of each state's government/secretary of state Website is given in the chapter on creating your own business. Click on the link for your state to learn more.

At times, *IMPACT* linked arms with other organizations that were already doing projects *(Operation Christmas Child, Meals-On-Wheels, Dress-A-Girl, Hearts and Horses)*. Other times, they created their own projects *(Random Acts of Christmas Kindness)*. You can do both things in your organization.

Some of the requirements for winning awards (either at school or for scholarships) involve having community service hours *outside of* school. Not all of your hours can be obtained through a group like Key Club, for example.

Our two remaining high school daughters are working to earn a Volunteer Cord to wear around their necks at graduation. The require-ment for *just* their senior year is 120 hours of volunteer work. Much of that has to be done with activities we plan ourselves. Having our own community service organization is a great way to accomplish that goal. **The judges like to see students who are true leaders in their commu-nity and who take the initiative to do things outside of school clubs.**

## WHAT'S UNDERLINE PASSION?

Are there things you're doing right now that you can include under the community service organization you create? Are you volunteering at the church nursery? Are you volunteering to scoop snow from your elderly neighbor's driveway? Are you donating items to the Humane Society? If you are, invite some friends to participate with you, and *voilà*! You now have a community service group! **Declare yourself a group, give everyone a position, plan some projects, start a Facebook page to document your activities and you are well on your way to doing something no one else is doing!**

*When you write your scholarship résumé and essay, be sure to include that you are the Founder of a community service organization. If you have a logo, put it on your résumé and essay letterhead. Create a business card with your name (as the Founder) on it and attach it to your résumé or scholarship application. If you have links to a Website or Facebook page, include those links on your business card, scholarship résumé or application. You will look like a real pro!*

How would **YOU** like to be the Founder and President of a community service organization? Doesn't that sound cool? It's a great way to demonstrate your leadership skills and take your volunteering to the next level.

If you're looking for great organizations to link arms with, here are some of our favorites: Dress-A-Girl Around the World, Operation Christmas Child, and Adaptive Adventures. I will tell you about each one in the following chapter.

# CHAPTER 6
## PARTNER ORGANIZATIONS

DRESS-A-GIRL AROUND THE WORLD
A WORLD WHERE EVERY GIRL HAS AT LEAST ONE NEW DRESS

*Dress-A-Girl Around the World* is a campaign under *Hope 4 Women International*, bringing dignity to women around the world since 2006. Their dream is for every girl to at least have one new dress. They want girls to know that they are worthy, loved and respected. The second picture below is of Katie, one of the members of our *IMPACT* group. She had the opportunity to go to Africa and take some of the dresses they sewed to give to the young girls. Katie said the girls were fighting over the dresses! They all wanted one. Often times, we don't have the privilege of seeing and experiencing the impact we've made in someone's life but when we do, it's magical.

A group of women in our church meets once a quarter to sew dresses, and members of *IMPACT* attend. The kids also take extra material home and work on the dresses together in their free time. If this is something you'd like to do, contact the organization to see how you can get started and how you can get the simple dress pattern. All you need to know is how to sew a straight line.

http://www.dressagirlaroundtheworld.com

# ✍ OPERATION CHRISTMAS CHILD
## GOOD NEWS. GREAT JOY.

# Operation Christmas Child
### A PROJECT *of* SAMARITAN'S PURSE

*Operation Christmas Child* is part of a national organization called Samaritan's Purse. Samaritan's Purse is a nondenominational evangelical Christian organization providing spiritual and physical aid to hurting people around the world.

There are a variety of ways you can volunteer with both Samaritan's Purse and Operation Christmas Child. You can purchase toys, school supplies, and hygiene items to pack into shoeboxes, or you can work at a Distribution Center processing boxes. *IMPACT* does both every year because it's so much fun. However, if you want to work at the Distribution Center, you need to sign up months ahead of time. Everyone seems to want to do it! We've even met families at the Distribution Center in Denver who fly in from other states to volunteer. Millions of boxes have been sent overseas to date.

Many churches have shoebox packing events where you can either donate items or help pack the shoeboxes with toys, school supplies or hygiene items. The kids in *IMPACT* raise their own money, go shopping, purchase the supplies, pack the boxes, and give them to a local church to deliver to the Distribution Center. The pick-up date for the boxes is by Thanksgiving.

To raise money this year to buy items for the shoeboxes, our *IMPACT* group is hosting Kitten Yoga! Whoever comes will make a donation to attend the class. All the funds will go directly to the cause and will enable the kids to go Christmas shopping for the little children overseas. Even though there will probably be more playing with the kittens than actual yoga happening, it will be a super fun way to raise money.

If you want to be part of this dynamic project, contact *Operation Christmas Child* to find a church near you that is participating. If you'd prefer to do it with a group of friends, they can give you information on how to go about it.

If you're like so many other "givers," you know the feeling that comes from giving to those who are less fortunate. Below is the link to help get you started making a difference in the life of a child.

https://www.samaritanspurse.org/what-we-do/operation-christmas-child/

## ✏️ BONUS TIP: HERE'S HOW OUR 12-YEAR OLD DAUGHTER WON THE KOHL'S SCHOLARSHIP...

In the Kohl's scholarship essay, we talked about *IMPACT*, the other service projects my daughter was involved with, as well as her academic achievements. However, we chose one project to discuss in depth. I think this was key to winning the Regional scholarship. We talked about the things she did personally and the things *Operation Christmas Child* did as a whole.

When Kohl's announced our daughter as the winner and did a press release on her, they quoted the stats that related to *Operation Christmas Child*. That year, *IMPACT* raised $390 by going door-to-door and collecting money to buy items to fill the shoeboxes. They filled 14 shoeboxes, which were then sent to a Distribution Center to be processed.

We are fortunate enough to live near one of the Distribution Centers, so the *IMPACT* group volunteered to process boxes. On an assembly line, each *IMPACT* member processed hundreds of boxes. The total number of boxes processed in 2014 at the Denver Distribution Center alone was 748,000. That's the number Kohl's seemed most interested in.

*IMPACT* was a very small part of something bigger. They personally contributed 14 out of 748,000 shoeboxes, but that was apparently enough to win the Regional Kohl's Scholarship. Note: When we wrote the essay, we included a lot of details. Remember, the scholarship judges like numbers.

The Kohl's scholarship is available for children as young as 8 years old. It's never too early to start looking for and applying for scholarships. The sooner you start your community service organization, business or big project, the better.

**THE TOP THREE SECRETS ARE SOMETHING YOU CAN DO REGARDLESS OF AGE, ACADEMIC GRADES OR EXPERIENCE. If you start early, that's great. If you start your senior year, that's great as well.** *Just start!*

One of the other winners of the Kohl's Scholarship was a young man who created an initiative to pass a bill in his local government. That's an interesting and unique thing to do as a high school student. It was certainly different from other essays I've read about, such as young people overcoming an illness or a traumatic past. It just goes to show that you can follow your passions, whatever they are, and win scholarship money.

## ✒ ADAPTIVE ADVENTURES
### FREEDOM THROUGH MOBILITY

Adaptive Adventures believes in Freedom Through Mobility. Their mission is to provide progressive outdoor sports opportunities to improve the quality of life for children, adults, and veterans with physical disabilities and their families. Go to their Website and watch the crazy, amazing video on their home page. You won't believe the things some of these people can do! Truly inspiring!

> *Strength does not come from physical capacity. It comes from an indomitable will. -Mohandas Gandhi*

If you don't have Adaptive Adventures in your area, consider offering an adaptive program for people at your local Recreation Center. If this is something you want to do, talk to your local recreation center representative about offering an adaptive program and/or classes through them via the community service group you created. You could offer sports events as well as art classes and/or social outings.

Heads up... if you offer programs through recreation centers, you need to provide your information several months in advance so they have time to print the class information in their advertising brochures/magazines.

https://adaptiveadventures.org/

## BEST. PROJECT. EVER.
### RANDOM ACTS OF CHRISTMAS KINDNESS

One of the most exciting projects *IMPACT* did was *Random Acts of Christmas Kindness*. The kids and their friends pooled their money together and hit the town looking for people to whom they could spread a little Christmas joy. If you start your own community service organization, this activity is a must! After doing this, you won't ever care if you win any scholarship money. The satisfaction from this project trumps anything of monetary value.

The kids filled Ziploc® bags with dollar bills and coins and included one of the colorful *Random Act of Christmas Kindness* cards. We found the cards online and printed them out on cardstock.

We also made labels that said, "You are the recipient of a Random Act of Christmas Kindness! Hope it makes you smile. Merry Christmas!" We then stuck them on the outside of the Ziplocs®.

The kids went from store to store and stuck the money-filled Ziplocs® onto whatever they could find... and then they hid and waited for the lucky recipients to discover them!

Ziploc® bags were stuck between toys in the toy section, on bubble gum machines, and on Redbox® machines. The kids even dropped some on the floor and watched as unsuspecting (and unobservant!) people walked right over them. It was fun to watch as people found them.

## ☞ OUR FAVORITE STORY

I remember standing in a long line at a checkout counter in Kohl's with some of the *IMPACT* kids and hearing a lady say, "Hey! Look what I found! It says I'm the recipient of a Random Act of Christmas Kindness."

To which someone else replied, "Me too! I found one of those, too!" Everyone waiting in line was watching and listening... intrigued by what was going on.

The first lady said, "I never get anything for myself. And look what I found!"

It was a dollar. *ONE MEASLY DOLLAR!* She was so excited to finally have something for herself. You never know what kind of impact you can have on someone else. We just stood in line, beaming, but not uttering a word!

At a couple different stores, we told the cashier that we were buying a restaurant gift card for someone, but we didn't know which one to get. We asked for their recommendation and asked which one *they* would most enjoy. We paid for the gift card and promptly handed it back to the cashier, telling them they were the recipient of a Random Act of Christmas Kindness. One of the cashiers was so touched that she walked all the way around the counter and gave us a BIG hug! It's been several years since that happened and she may have forgotten all about it, but we never will!

You can create some incredible memories and have a lot of fun when you step outside of your comfort zone and do something nice for someone else.

**Other ideas include:**

- Paying for someone's meal at a fast food restaurant
- Paying for someone's toll behind you
- Putting extra money in a parking meter
- Leaving coins and little boxes of detergent at the laundry mat
- Making hot chocolate and giving it to outdoor workers in the winter
- Giving cold bottles of water or ice cream treats to outdoor workers on hot summer days

Stories like these make impressive scholarship essays. Go out and create some stories!

## CHAPTER 7
### SECRET 2

### ✏ BECOME A BUSINESS OWNER

The second scholarship hacking secret is to create a business and become a business owner. Like founding your own community service organization, becoming a business owner is actually pretty easy. You aren't required to make a ton of money in your business or work a ton of hours in order to win scholarships. **The fact that you started a business sets you apart from everyone working at the local fast food chain.**

**Here are the steps to creating your own business:**

1. *Create a Product or Service*
2. *Form a Limited Liability Company (LLC)*
3. *Brand Yourself*
4. *Get to Work*

A lot of students who are seniors and are just learning the scholarship hacking secrets choose this secret to implement. Many of them are already doing side jobs that they can easily and quickly turn into an official business. You will learn how to do that in the following chapters.

## CREATE A PRODUCT OR SERVICE: WHAT'S YOUR BIG IDEA?

When you start a business, it's best to figure out what peoples' needs are and create a business or product to meet those needs. If you can't figure something out, do whatever you love doing. Think about what you're already doing, or come up with something new.

The following is a list to give you some business ideas:

- Babysitting / Child Care service
- House sitting service
- Pet business
- Lawn business
- Housecleaning business
- Making a product and selling it on Etsy
- Selling Grandma's Secret Jelly recipe at the Farmer's Market
- Giving music/art/dance lessons
- Tutoring younger students
- Writing an e-book and selling it online
- Offering a gig on Fiverr
- Teaching elderly people how to use the computer
- Teaching elderly people how to operate their cell phones
- Teaching exercise classes at retirement homes
- Teaching art lessons to developmentally challenged children and adults

## CRAZY IDEA

There was a guy on *Shark Tank* who drew personalized cats for people. His business was called "I Want to Draw a Cat For You." His cat drawings literally looked like stick figures! He charged customers $9.95 in exchange for custom drawings of cats that Steve Gadlin would draw to the customer's specifications.

Gadlin first came up with the idea as a joke, with the goal of seeing if he could construct a successful business using only a widget. At first, his Website consisted of only a YouTube video and Paypal button. The business became well-known after Gadlin appeared on Shark Tank to promote it. He persuaded Mark Cuban to invest $25,000 in his idea. Gadlin drew 18,794 cat pictures before he closed his company.

## COOL TECH IDEA

When my son was in high school, he created a graphics design business called SkyBlue to design Websites and logos. He chose a name for the business, created an LLC, designed his own logo, and made business cards. When he wrote his essay, he put his logo on the letterhead. It looked impressive. I'm sure it caught the eye of more than one judge.

## BRILLIANT IDEA

I heard a story about a 12-year-old who cleaned his neighbor's garbage cans with a power sprayer. He set people up on a "subscription" order to clean their cans every month for $25 per month. His customers were instructed to set their cans out on a certain day of the month and "he" would clean them and set them back. Actually, he "employed" some of his friends, and *they* did the work! He paid them a certain dollar amount per can cleaned, and he kept the rest of the money. He just oversaw the operation and cashed the checks! He ended up selling his business and making a lot of money. Smart kid!

## ENTREPRENEURSHIP AT ITS BEST

My nephew, Noah Schulman, did something similar beginning when he was just ten years old. He wanted to have his own cash to buy things so he started his own lawn business. The only problem was... he was too small to operate the weed eater. This minor detail didn't stop Noah though! He hired a couple older teenage boys to trim the weeds and he cut the lawns. When he started his business, he charged $30 per lawn and paid his first employee $10 and kept the rest. Noah saved up his money and eventually bought a riding lawn mower. He's served over 30 customers, earned thousands of dollars, had employees, and is now saving to buy a vehicle. Quite an accomplishment for someone who's only 16 years old. Noah is a great example of someone who sets their mind to something, and despite the obstacles, is an American success.

When he was young, he also sold chilled water bottles to construction workers in his neighborhood. He hired one of his buddies to pull the wagon filled with the water bottles, and he did all the talking and conducted the sale. He sold each water bottle for $1 and paid his friend ten cents for each bottle they sold. He was making a great profit until his parents noticed all the water bottles missing from their fridge! He eventually started purchasing his own bottles of water and then upgraded to flavored water. Noah's story proves that anyone is capable of accomplishing their dreams with enough innovation, dedication, and strong work ethic.

## ☞ TURN YOUR GIG INTO A BIZ

Think about what kind of jobs you're doing right now. Are you babysitting? Are you mowing lawns? Are you teaching music lessons to kids? Are you house sitting? Are you animal sitting? Do you like designing Websites? *WHATEVER YOU'RE CURRENTLY DOING, TURN IT INTO AN OFFICIAL BUSINESS!* Even if you're a senior and you're beginning to apply for scholarships, it's not too late to start. Many of the students in our Secret Scholarship Club are starting their businesses as seniors. Of all three Scholarship Secrets, this one seems to be the favorite.

It will look great on your résumé or scholarship application when you say that you are a BUSINESS OWNER! There are only a few extra steps you need to take to become an official business as opposed to "just doing odd jobs." This applies to any type of business you create.

## WHY MAKE IT OFFICIAL?

**Forming an official business will set you apart from other students who are doing the same types of jobs.** It takes a little extra work and know-how, but it shows you are the type of person who goes above and beyond, takes leadership roles, and wants to contribute to society in a much bigger way.

You might be thinking that you don't have time to start a business. One of the girls in our Secret Scholarship Club thought that too, because she was already a senior. But then Savannah decided to take the plunge and do something she's always wanted to do... create a blog. She formed a business called Cherished Ink - Choosing Authenticity, and she went to work! She started by forming an LLC and getting a Website. Now she's inspiring readers with her creative writing.

Another girl in our club felt overwhelmed by the thought of making her business official, but then Katie realized she was already teaching flute lessons to kids, so she might as well spend a little extra time and turn her work into an official business. The hardest part of creating her business was thinking of a name. We searched the Internet for ideas but only came across boring ideas such as "So-and-So's Flute Academy." Katie was hoping for something more original so we flipped through some CDs on my bookshelf and found Rogers and Hammerstein's *The Sound of Music* soundtrack. Katie immediately fell in love with it and decided to call her flute business *Sounds of Music, LLC*. She checked the Secretary of State Website to see if the name was available and sure enough, it was! Her next step was designing business cards and flyers to gather more customers and thinking about what other "services" she could offer. We came up with doing mini-recitals for her students' families and performing at local retirement centers (as a volunteer project).

Andrew had done a variety of different work projects such as mowing lawns, helping people move, and house sitting. I encouraged him to form a handy-man business and turn it into an LLC. He was so excited about the idea that he decided to create two businesses! Because he was an accomplished pianist, he thought he could give piano lessons to younger students. At first, he was worried about his teaching abilities, but I reminded him that he knew more than beginner students and would do great. You can teach if you're at least one step ahead of your students!

Think about the different things you've done as jobs. Is there something you've always wanted to do but haven't started yet, like Savannah? Is there something you're doing right now that you can just turn into an LLC like Katie did? Or are there a variety of jobs you've done and you plan to continue doing that you can create a business from like Andrew did?

The power of creating a business is this… when Savannah, Katie, and Andrew fill out their scholarship résumés, they can say they're the founder and owner of an actual business. Meanwhile, all their peers are saying they babysat, mowed lawns, or worked at a fast food restaurant as their form of employment. *Do you see the difference becoming an official business makes? Would you agree that when the scholarship judges look at Savannah, Katie, and Andrew, they will see leaders?*

Here's what Katie's scholarship résumé looks like as the owner of a company:

**EMPLOYMENT HISTORY**
**Founder and Owner of *Sounds of Music, LLC*** *(2017-present)*

- Taught flute lessons to children ages 7-12
- Taught Theory Music
- Conducted "mini" recitals for students' families
- Performed at three local retirement centers

That looks more impressive than her peers' scholarship résumés that look like this:

**EMPLOYMENT HISTORY**

- Babysat children ages one to nine years old
- Mowed laws for the neighbors

*If I told you the specific steps necessary to create a business and told you it only takes about 15 minutes, do you think you could do it?* Sounds easy enough, right? During one of our Secret Scholarship Club meetings, I helped Savannah set up an LLC, and then she helped some of the other students do the same. It's that easy!

## HOW CAN I TURN MY BUSINESS INTO AN LLC?

After you decide what product or service you'd like to offer, make your business official by turning it into an LLC. After you do that, you will create a *tagline* to go with the name you chose.

When considering a new business venture, think about what the business should be called. The name of your business is important because it identifies who you are and allows your customers to remember you. You will want to protect your business name. This is accomplished by completing the vital first step of creating a business, which is to **register the chosen name with the Secretary of State and confirm that the name is available**. A business name is only protected when it is approved and filed with the Secretary of State.

To make sure the name you want is available in your state, you need to go to your state's Website. Depending on the state, you will need to find either the official state Website or the secretary of state Website. I've included a list of all the states' Websites at the end of this chapter so you can quickly and easily find yours.

## FOLLOW ALONG TO LEARN HOW

If you are reading the e-book version of this book, you can click on the (Colorado Secretary of State) link and follow along as I walk you through the steps of searching for and filing a business name: http://www.sos.state.co.us/

1. Click BUSINESS, TRADEMARKS, TRADE NAMES
2. Click NAME AVAILABILITY SEARCH. Type in the name you would like to call your business. Include the abbreviation (LLC, Ltd, or Inc). Click SEARCH. If the name is not available, try something similar. If it is available, congratulations!
3. Click on CLICK HERE TO FILE A DOCUMENT
4. Under FILE A FORM, choose the abbreviation you want to use. Limited liability company (LLC) is a good one to use
5. Type in the exact name you want to use (with the abbreviation)
6. Fill out the ARTICLES OF ORGANIZATION
7. Pay the fee; You are now officially a business! *#yourock!*

## PERIODIC REPORT FILING

Each year, you will need to go back to the state Website and do a **PERIODIC REPORT FILING** for a small fee to make sure everything is accurate and updated. In Colorado, the fee is only $10. They will send you an email each year, letting you know when you need to "File a Report" (which basically means look over your information and pay the fee).

## EMPLOYER IDENTIFICATION NUMBER (EIN)

You will be given an EIN to use on your taxes. **SAVE THIS NUMBER! IT IS IMPORTANT!** If you make over $600, you will have to pay taxes on your earnings. However, there is a whole list of things you can write off so you don't have to pay as much tax. Having your own business and using legal tax write-offs is one of the secrets of the rich.

## TAX DEDUCTIONS

Some of the things you can write off are mileage, cell phone, Internet service, meals and entertainment related to your business (50%), and more. A simple Google search will give you deduction ideas, or you can talk to an accountant about it. At the end of the year a Schedule C, which lists your income and expenses, will be completed by you or your tax accountant. The resulting number will then go on your Form 1040 as your self-employment income for the year.

## 📜 WHAT TO LOOK FOR ON YOUR STATE'S WEBSITE

**When you go to your state's Website, search around for the following phrases (or something similar to them):**

- Search for a Business Entity
- Search our Database
- Business Name Search
- Corporations
- Business
- Business Services
- Start a Business

Click on whatever you find and continue to follow the steps they give.

If you need help setting up an LLC, ask a banker at your local bank and he or she may be able to help you set it up.

## 📜 HERE IS A LIST OF WEBSITES FOR EACH STATE:

1. Alabama: http://sos.alabama.gov/
2. Alaska: http://alaska.gov/businessHome.html
3. Arizona: https://www.azsos.gov/business
4. Arkansas: http://www.sos.arkansas.gov/Pages/default.aspx
5. California: http://www.sos.ca.gov/
6. Colorado: http://www.sos.state.co.us/
7. Connecticut: http://search-sos.org/connecticut-co-business-entity-corporation-search/
8. Delaware: http://corp.delaware.gov/

9. Florida: http://dos.myflorida.com/
10. Georgia: http://sos.ga.gov/index.php/corporations
11. Hawaii: http://cca.hawaii.gov/breg/
12. Idaho: https://sos.idaho.gov/corp/index.html
13. Illinois: http://www.cyberdriveillinois.com/departments/business_services/home.html
14. Indiana: https://inbiz.in.gov/BOS/Home/Index
15. Iowa: https://sos.iowa.gov/
16. Kansas: http://kssos.org/
17. Kentucky: https://www.sos.ky.gov/Pages/default.aspx
18. Louisiana: http://www.sos.la.gov/Pages/default.aspx
19. Maine: http://maine.gov/sos/cec/corp/index.html
20. Maryland: https://www.secstates.com/MD_Maryland_Secretary_of_State_Corporation_Search
21. Massachusetts: http://www.sec.state.ma.us/
22. Michigan: http://www.michigan.gov/sos/0,4670,7-127-1631---,00.html
23. Minnesota: http://www.sos.state.mn.us/
24. Mississippi: http://www.sos.ms.gov/Pages/default.aspx
25. Missouri: http://sos.mo.gov/
26. Montana: http://sos.mt.gov/
27. Nebraska: http://www.sos.ne.gov/dyindex.html
28. Nevada: http://secretaryofstates.com/nevada/
29. New Hampshire: http://sos.nh.gov/
30. New Jersey: http://secretaryofstates.com/new-jersey/
31. New Mexico: http://www.sos.state.nm.us/
32. New York: http://secretaryofstates.com/new-york/
33. North Carolina: https://www.nc.gov/services-info/starting-business-nc
34. North Dakota: http://sos.nd.gov/business/business-services
35. Ohio: https://www.sos.state.oh.us/
36. Oklahoma: https://www.sos.ok.gov/
37. Oregon: http://sos.oregon.gov/business/Pages/register.aspx
38. Pennsylvania: http://www.dos.pa.gov/BusinessCharities/Business/Pages/default.aspx
39. Rhode Island: http://sos.ri.gov/divisions/business-portal
40. South Carolina: http://scsos.com/

41. South Dakota: https://sdsos.gov/businessservices/corporations/default.aspx
42. Tennessee: http://sos.tn.gov/
43. Texas: http://www.sos.state.tx.us/
44. Utah: https://corporations.utah.gov/
45. Vermont: https://www.sec.state.vt.us/corporationsbusiness-services.aspx
46. Virginia: https://sccefile.scc.virginia.gov/
47. Washington: https://www.sos.wa.gov/corps/Forms.aspx
48. West Virginia: http://www.sos.wv.gov/Pages/default.aspx
49. Wisconsin: http://www.wisconsin.gov/Pages/home.aspx
50. Wyoming: http://soswy.state.wy.us/business/

# CHAPTER 8
## THE NUTS AND BOLTS

## ✐ WHAT DOES IT MEAN TO BRAND YOURSELF?

Branding yourself is the fun part of creating your business. Branding means leaving a mark or an impression. It's a way to create a certain image for yourself and for your business.

1. What do you want your business to look like?
2. How do you want it to feel?
3. What do you want people to think of when they think of your business?
4. What do you want to be known for? *"The customer is always right."* *"We deliver the fastest." "We put your needs first." "You can trust us."*
5. What impression do you want to leave?

You can reveal what your brand is by creating taglines, logos, Websites, business cards and other fun paraphernalia.

## ✐ CREATE A TAGLINE

After you choose a name for your business, choose a tagline to go along with it. **A tagline is a few catchy words that describe your business**. How many of these taglines do you recognize?

- A Diamond is Forever *(De Beers Diamond Company)*
- Just Do It *(Nike)*
- Where's the Beef? *(Wendy's)*
- Great Taste. Less Filling *(Miller Brewing Company)*
- Don't Leave Home Without It *(American Express)*
- Melts in Your Mouth, Not in Your Hand *(M&Ms)*
- You're in Good Hands *(Allstate)*
- We Try Harder *(Avis)*

Taglines are a fun way to let people know what your business is all about. What can you come up with for yours?

## CREATE A LOGO

If you have the ability, or if you know someone who could help you, create a logo for your business. You can put it on business cards, letterheads, t-shirts, pens, etc. A good place to start for creating a logo is Fiverr. It is a place where, starting at $5, people will provide different services for you. The logos always end up costing more than $5, depending on what you want, but it's a good place to begin. When you go to Fiverr, click GRAPHICS AND DESIGN > LOGO DESIGN

https://www.fiverr.com/

## CREATE A WEBSITE

Create a Website or business Facebook page if you think it will enhance your business. An inexpensive hosting site is BlueHost. They are the #1 recommended Web hosting by Wordpress.org. Their beginner packages are only a few dollars per month. Other inexpensive Website options are Weebley, WIX, and GoDaddy.

https://www.bluehost.com/

## CREATE BUSINESS CARDS AND OTHER FUN STUFF

Make flyers and business cards (through Vistaprint.com) to hand out and drum up business. If you have a logo, you can put it on your flyers, business cards, stationery, etc.

Vistaprint.com is an incredible company with inexpensive services. You can literally buy 100 business cards for $5. They have hundreds of pre-designed templates you can choose from, or you can upload your own logo. Check them out! They will get you set up and feeling like a proud business owner quickly.

http://www.vistaprint.com/

Branding yourself, creating logos and Websites, and handing out business cards are the types of things business owners do. All of these activities will show the scholarship judges (as well as future employers) that you have the leadership skills, self-discipline, and initiative it takes to be successful.

## PROMOTE YOUR BUSINESS

Start promoting yourself and your business. Offer discounts and free trial services/products. Make your customers feel like they are getting a great deal, and they will keep coming back for more. Keep track of the time you spend, the money you make, the services you provide, and the people you help. This is important information to include in a scholarship essay. Remember, the scholarship judges like details and numbers. It is a representation of how much you are doing.

If you've provided incredible service for someone, ask if they will write a recommendation letter for you. Letters like this are especially important to have to attach to résumés and scholarship applications.

# CHAPTER 9
## SECRET 3

 **BECOME A PROJECT MANAGER**

The third scholarship hacking secret is to become a Project Manager and concentrate all your efforts on completing and managing one big project. The advantage of this is that you will have a bigger impact by not spreading yourself thin doing a lot of little projects. Your "numbers" will be bigger, and you will grow as a leader exponentially. You will also reach more people. The more time you spend on something, the more of an expert you will become. You will have more stories to tell because you have built a strong foundation and a strong network.

## HOW WILL DOING A BIG PROJECT IMPRESS THE SCHOLARSHIP JUDGES?

Project Managers are leaders. Leaders are people who can visualize a project and carry it through to completion. A leader must be organized and persistent until the job is done. There may be obstacles along the way, but a leader proves his or her bravery by gracefully tackling whatever comes his or her way.

A Project Manager is also a delegator. A delegator is someone who hands off pieces of a project to another person and ensures that the work gets done properly. Being able to do these things shows strength of character, and that is exactly what scholarship judges are looking for when they're choosing a winner.

**One of the things that will set you apart from other students is your ability to execute a big project while maintaining strength in other areas of your life.**

## WHAT KIND OF PROJECT SHOULD I CHOOSE?

Think about something you are passionate about... something you love doing. Turn that into a project. When you're doing something you love, you will stay motivated to continue on when the going gets tough. Your excitement will carry you. If a member of *IMPACT* wanted to do this, he or she could choose one of the projects we've done and then do that ten-fold. So instead of sewing a few dresses for impoverished girls overseas, that person could concentrate on sewing 50 or 100 dresses. That would catch the scholarship judge's attention for sure.

## EAGLE LEADERSHIP SERVICE PROJECT

Doing an Eagle Leadership Service Project for the Boys Scouts is a great example of focusing on one big project. I love the way the Boy Scouts organization describes the purpose of doing the project...

> *"The purpose of the project is to give you a personal, direct way to demonstrate to your Board of Review that you have leadership skills. The service delivered, while important, is sort of a bonus. As you consider project ideas ask yourself, "How will this allow me to demonstrate leadership?" The answers to that question will require recruiting some helpers, giving them specific tasks to do, providing them with instructions so that they know their*

*jobs, coordinating the preparations and work so that everything gets done, and monitoring the work so that it is done satisfactorily. You could do a service project by yourself, but you can't do an Eagle Leadership Service Project without leading other people."*

Here are some Eagle Scout project ideas gleaned from an online source that may give you some ideas for your project (http://www.eaglescout.org/project/select.html). I like these ideas because they are unique. The advantage of managing a project is that you don't need to have a 4.0 GPA to do it. You just need to have leadership skills, organization, and grit. Isn't that what businesses want in a Project Manager anyway?

A lot of students tend to do the same type of projects and write about the same things in scholarship essays, like serving in a soup kitchen. If you do something like that, you need to work it like a job and dedicate about 100 hours per year doing it. Some of the following projects didn't take a large amount of time. The objective here, however, is to come up with an idea of your own and spend a significant amount of time and effort on it to make it happen. **Think:** *Big Project. Big Impact.*

## ✍ PROJECT IDEAS FROM A VARIETY OF STUDENTS:

- **Voting Booths:** I made three voting booths for our town hall in Topsham, Vermont. One of them was a booth for handicapped voters.

- **Youth Protection and Identification Program:** I provided parents and children with information to prevent abductions. I also provided a place for parents to fingerprint and videotape their child in case they ever need to file a missing child report.

- **Community Bicycle Registration:** The number of bicycle thefts in our area was rising, so I worked with the Police to develop a card file where people could register their bikes. For three Saturdays, we put on a bike safety and registration fair.

- **Built a Playground:** There is a home for orphans in our neighborhood. I organized a construction project and built a playground in their backyard for the kids.

- **Tiger Shelter at Wildlife Preserve:** The tiger shelters at a local animal preserve were falling apart, so I organized a project to rebuild the shelters over the cages.

- **Built Picnic Tables for Park:** We built new picnic tables for the park's pavilions.

- **Leadership Training Program:** My school district has a neat leadership training program, so I helped them organize and train the staff members for a week-long retreat for the 6th graders.

- **Eyeglass Drive:** I collected eyeglasses from local mortuaries for three months, and then sent them with a doctor who goes to Mexico. He gave them to people who could not afford to buy glasses for themselves.

- **Homeless Shelter Concert:** I play in a rock band. To help stock the shelves of the homeless shelter, I organized a concert where the admission price was a can of food.

- **Bicycle Racks for Baseball Complex:** The grass was torn up at our baseball diamond because kids kept dumping their bikes on the ground. I got a construction company to donate the materials and built a cement bike rack on the edge of the field.

- **Hearing Aid Drive:** I heard about the eyeglass drive, where Scouts collect eyeglasses from local mortuaries and send them to third world countries. I decided to try it with hearing aids. I worked with an audiologist (my dad) to get the project going.

- **Restore Storage Shed at Neighborhood Park:** The shed at our neighborhood park had been ignored for a long time. I got our troop and neighborhood together to repair it.

- **Cemetery Directory:** I cataloged all of the gravestones in our city cemetery. Then I worked with the troop to put together a cemetery kiosk where visitors could look at a large map and find the graves they wanted to visit.

- **Recycling Drive:** I live in a city where there is a lot of trash in the streets. After the 4th of July Parade, I organized my troop and some neighborhood groups to clean up all the trash along the parade route. We sorted it for recycling.

- **Toy Drive For Christmas:** I organized a toy drive with a thrift store in town. All the toys were donated to foster homes and orphanages.

- **Cut Down Trees for Firewood:** There was an old orchard in my neighborhood. I organized my troop to go and cut down the dead trees, and we delivered the wood to widows for firewood.

- **Flood Sandbags:** In spring the river near our town flooded. I organized groups to fill sandbags to protect the buildings along the river.

- **Area Trail Maintenance:** A public trail was in need of some improvements so I put in two grade-level steps to prevent erosion. I also cleaned the trail and leveled it in places.

- **Built Large Shelving Units in the Interfaith Ministries Food Pantry:** This was an all-day affair for about 8-10 scouts.

- **Built Bat Boxes and Owl Houses:** Working with Sam Houston National Forest, one of our Eagles built bat boxes. One weekend we built them. The next weekend we went on a campout to the national forest and put out the boxes. We had a great time.

- **Built Trash Receptacles:** Built trash receptacles for the local nature center and installed them.

- **Built Benches in the Rest Areas Along a Nature Trail:** The park ranger has a shopping list of things that need to be done.

- **Recruited Volunteers for Food Bank**: Recruited volunteers from the Troop and high school service clubs (including getting formal permission through high school channels) and managed their work at the Community Food Bank of New Jersey.

- **Put Together a Door-to-Door Clothing Drive**

- **Plant and Shrub Identification:** Hung signs on trees and cemented them on the ground next to plants or shrubs to identify what they were.

- **Cleaned Up and Repaired Headstones in an Old Community Cemetery:** Ten or so Scouts for two full days of work + adults.

- **Built a Walking Trail Around a Lake in a Local County Park:** Requires a LOT of patience working with the county government. The full trail was two projects. About four workdays with 4-6 boys and adults each day for each half.

- **Worked on Walking/Nature Trails**: Project done at local schools. Several days with various sized crews of 5-10.

- **Constructed and Installed a Guide Rope and Braille Signs for a Boardwalk at a Local Nature Center:** Nature centers always seem to have projects for Eagle Scouts.

- **Cleaned and Repainted the Parking Lot for a Large Local Church**

- **Installed a basketball goal and 1/2 court marking at a nearby church parking lot as a recreational project for the church and community youth.**

- **Planned and Executed a Large Concrete Sidewalk Pour at a Church**: Digging, leveling and forming up for the pour was quite a bit of planning and work and was a rather educational experience for the several scouts that had been recruited to work on the project. It took several days.

- **Built Bagging Tables for a Local Volunteer Organization**

- **Built Cages for the Humane Society**

- **Painted Church Interior:** Painted the interior of a two-story local church Sunday school building.

- **Moved School Supplies:** Moved the shelving, supplies, stock, and books from a stockroom in a 500-pupil elementary school to a new storage building.

- **Tree Removal and Replacement:** Dug up and removed several dead trees, planted replacement trees and some new trees along the access road to a local neighborhood, and planted bushes and fixed up several existing nursery beds.

- **Painted House Numbers:** Painted house numbers on the curb for each house in a 700-home development.

- **Cleared and Developed a Nature Trail at a Local Park**

- **Created a Fitness Trail:** Laid a wood chip trail around a local schoolyard for the students and citizens to use as a fitness trail.

- **Painted Firehouse Walls:** Painted the inside walls of a firehouse

- **Refurbished Caboose at a Museum:** Refurbished the inside of a Chessie System caboose that the town purchased for a local museum.

## 🎓 WHEN YOU WRITE YOUR SCHOLARSHIP ESSAY DESCRIBING THE PROJECT, INCLUDE THE FOLLOWING:

1. Your personal reason for doing the project
2. The number of hours you spent
3. The number of students and adults you recruited to join you
4. The steps you took to complete the project
5. What tasks you delegated to others
6. The obstacles you overcame and how you overcame them
7. The results you achieved (who was impacted, how many people were impacted, how they were impacted, personal quotes from the people impacted)
8. The highlights of executing the project; your favorite part of doing the project
9. How you grew and changed as a person as a result of creating and leading the project

**Remember to call yourself a Project Manager in your scholarship résumé and essay.** When you create your résumé, put your title as Project Manager, list the location and dates you were involved, and make a bulleted list of specific things you did to organize and execute the project. Include as many details, specifications, and numbers as you can. Create a business card with your name and title and include that with your résumé or scholarship applications. Let the scholarship judges know you mean business!

One of the students in our Scholarship Club organized and led a group of students to Texas to assist in cleanup efforts after Hurricane Harvey. Rather than just putting this down on his résumé as one of the activities he did, I encouraged him to call himself a Project Manager because what he did was actually really impressive. His actions earned him the title. I felt Reece needed to be recognized for his incredible efforts, and this was the perfect way to do that. I wanted to make sure the scholarship judges could easily and clearly see everything Reece did.

To show you how cool this is, here's how Reece articulated his efforts on his scholarship résumé:

**COMMUNITY SERVICE PROJECTS**
*City, State*                                                    *August 2017*
**Frontier for Harvey – Project Manager and Founder**
Project Manager and Founder of the youth mission trip to Houston *(2017)*

- Raised money by organizing bake sales to donate to Samaritan's Purse and help pay for our travel expenses
- Advertised the project and recruited 20 students and chaperones
- Organized three meetings to explain practical details
- Compiled all information about participants in an Excel spreadsheet
- Collaborated with Samaritan's Purse to organize volunteer work, housing, and meals
- Researched and purchased inexpensive group flights ($180 round trip, per person)
- Assigned Key Club members at my high school the task of arranging a supply drive

*Isn't that awesome?* Do you think you could do the same with some of the things you're already doing in the community? Part of the secret is knowing how to present yourself and your activities on the résumé. This is the perfect way to do it. Becoming a Project Manager demonstrates leadership, motivation and organization at a whole new level!

# CHAPTER 10
## APPLYING FOR SCHOLARSHIPS

### THE NITTY GRITTY

After you decide which one (or more) of the top three secrets you want to implement, it's important to understand the nuts and bolts of applying for scholarships. In the following chapter, I will go over some of the basics to get you started on the right foot.

### BE ORGANIZED

Keep track of your activities and hours. As I mentioned before, log them in your phone as a quick and easy way to keep track of them. Periodically, jot them down in a notebook or in an Excel spreadsheet or Word document that you keep on your computer. A great app to use to keep track of your volunteer hours is *Track It Forward*. The National Honor Society even uses that one!

Keep all of your essays and applications in a file cabinet or in a folder on your computer desktop. When you are applying for different scholarships, you can copy and paste parts of applications you have previously written and use them for new ones. This alone will save you a lot of time and effort, and it will make applying for scholarships faster and easier. Make a separate folder for the following important items:

- Scholarship Résumé
- Transcripts
- Recommendation Letters
- Essays
- *Volunteer Hours* Spreadsheet
- *Colleges Applied for* Spreadsheet
- *Scholarships Applied for* Spreadsheet

Plan your projects ahead of time. Know how many hours you want to accomplish and begin to schedule your projects for the year. Don't let summer or school breaks slip by without scheduling in community service projects. If you are shooting for 100 hours of volunteer service per year, you will need to schedule the projects throughout the year on weekends, school breaks and during the summer. This is the only way to complete that many hours, especially if you are involved with sports, music, drama, church activities or other clubs.

Have everything you need before you start applying for scholarships. This includes the following:

- Scholarship Résumé
- Scholarship Essay
- Transcript
- Recommendation Letters
- Personal Website
- Business Card to attach to scholarship applications
- Resources such as *The Ultimate Scholarship Book, Scholarship Search Secrets,* and *Strengthsfinder 2.0*
- Community Service Organization, Business or Big Project that you are executing
- File Box
- Digital File Box/Folder on your computer desktop to keep track of your paperwork

- Notebook, Spreadsheet, or Word Document to keep track of your activities, hours, and awards
- Notebook, Spreadsheet, or Word Document to keep track of scholarships applied for and scholarships won
- Thank you cards to send to scholarship committees for scholarships won

## GET RECOMMENDATION LETTERS

Get two to three recommendation letters from the following list of people. Often times, college and scholarship applications only require one letter of recommendation, but it's nice to be able to choose the best one to include. If one is required, I suggest going above and beyond and giving them two.

- Teacher
- Principal
- School guidance counselor
- Employer
- Pastor
- Youth group leader
- Club leaders
- Volunteer/Community Service leaders
- Coach
- Camp Counselor
- Long-time friend of the family

This is an important aspect of applying for scholarships. At times, you will need to attach a letter of recommendation. Remember to ask for the letter well in advance of the time you need it. Many teachers are inundated with requests and need time to write a thoughtful letter for you. Provide them with your scholarship résumé so they have something to reference. We always like to give the people who write recommendation letters a gift card to show our appreciation for their kindness. If you are unable to do this, a nice thank you note would be appreciated.

# ✏ WRITE A SCHOLARSHIP RÉSUMÉ

A Scholarship Résumé is similar to a job résumé, but it also includes all of your activities, leadership roles, and awards.

The Scholarship Résumé will give the judges a complete look at who you are and what you've accomplished with one glance. When you write your scholarship *essay*, you won't have to waste valuable word count including all these things. You will be able to focus on telling a story and letting the judges get to know you that way. Remember to say you are a Founder, Owner, President or Project Manager whenever applicable.

**The Scholarship Résumé should include the following:**

- College Education Objective / Career Objective
- Employment History
- Community Volunteer Work
- School Activities / Clubs / Sports
- Leadership Roles
- Extracurricular Activities
- Awards
- Skills
- Education including GPA, Class Rank, AP or College classes taken, ACT/SAT scores, Expected Graduation Date
- Link to Personal Website, LinkedIn, Facebook or other social media site that showcases who you are and what you've accomplished

# ✏ USE RESOURCES

*Resource #1: The Ultimate Scholarship Book* **by Gen and Kelly Tanabe**

A great resource to use when applying for scholarships is *The Ultimate Scholarship Book* by Gen and Kelly Tanabe. This scholarship guide boasts of billions of dollars in scholarships, grants, and prizes. It also gives insider advice on how to win scholarships. The book is updated each year with hundreds and hundreds of pages of scholarships that you can apply for. You can purchase it on Amazon for less than $20.

### Resource #2: Colleges

Another great resource is the **college** you are applying to. They have a general application that you fill out with opportunities for additional scholarships. All you have to do is answer a couple essay questions per scholarship you apply for, and voila! You're done. That is how Jenna won her biggest scholarship. Each year they offer new ones; some you can't get until you are a sophomore, junior, or senior, or unless you are in a certain field of study. Stay involved in clubs and groups while you are in college so you can add those things to your résumé and application.

### Resource #3: The Community

The **community** also offers a variety of scholarships. Your local high school will also inform students of opportunities in the community. We've had the best success applying for scholarships through the college and the community. In fact, that's where all my children have received most of their scholarship monies. The local scholarships seem easier to win, as compared to the national ones or those advertised online.

### Civic Organizations

**The following is a list of civic organizations where you can inquire about scholarship opportunities:**

- Altrusa
- American Legion and American Legion Auxiliary
- American Red Cross
- Association of Junior Leagues International
- Boys and Girls Clubs
- Boy Scouts and Girl Scouts
- Circle K

- Civitan
- Elks Club
- Lions Club
- 4-H Clubs
- Fraternal Order of Eagles
- Friends of the Library
- Kiwanis International
- Knights of Columbus
- National Exchange Club
- National Grange
- Optimist International
- Performing Arts Center
- Rotary Club
- Rotaract and Interact
- Ruritan
- Sertoma International
- U.S. Jaycees
- USA Freedom Corps
- Veterans of Foreign Wars
- YMCA and YWCA
- Zonta International

*More Community Resources*

**Remember to also check the following places for scholarship opportunities. *The Ultimate Scholarship Book* goes into detail about each one. I highly recommend getting the book.**

- Local businesses
- Your parents' employer
- Your parents' or grandparents' military service
- Your employer
- Your parents' union
- Interest clubs; Community Organizations and Foundations
- Professional sports teams
- Church or religious organizations

- Local government
- Local newspapers
- The Internet; Google searches for local and national scholarships
- Professional associations
- Big businesses; Big Box stores like Walmart or other local businesses
- Well-known companies like Pepsi
- Colleges (Any college you apply for)
- Your high school as well as other high schools; High school counselor's office; High school bulletin boards
- Twitter, Facebook or other social media sites
- *The Ultimate Scholarship Book* by Gen and Kelly Tanabe

### Resource #4: *Scholarship Search Secrets* Sixth Edition by Christopher S. Penn

In my scholarship research, one of the best resources I found for information was *Scholarship Search Secrets* Sixth Edition by Christopher S. Penn. He gives some unique tips in there that you will find helpful. The resource is *free* so I recommend getting it.

Here is the link for you to download the e-book.

https://www.studentscholarshipsearch.com/ebook/

### Resource #5: *Strengthsfinder 2.0* by Tom Rath

Have you ever looked at yourself in the mirror and wondered if you really have any talents? Does it sometimes feel like you're just the average Joe? Or do you know what you're good at but you don't really know how to make a career out of it?

We discovered a great resource for helping you discover your gifts, talents and strengths. *Strengthsfinder 2.0* is an easy-to-read book, and you get to take a short quiz to uncover who you are. When you buy the book, you're given an access code to take the test. The findings are unique, personal and help you to understand yourself better. Once you get your results, you can add them to your scholarship essay under *Abilities* and *Skills*. It's important to know who you are and what you're good at so you can confidently present yourself to other people... whether they're scholarship judges or future employers.

You can get *Strengthsfinder 2.0* here:
http://www.strengthsfinder.com/home.aspx
http://www.tomrath.org/

### Resource #6:

Perhaps the best resource I've discovered is *All the Wisdom and None of the Junk – Secrets of Applying for College Admission and Scholarships* by Katy Craig and Katie Kramer. This easy-to-use guide gives readers the techniques they need to excel on applications by walking them through actual prompts and sample responses.

My daughter, Krista, was chosen to apply for a prestigious scholarship in our state, and this book alone gave us exactly what we needed to know to answer the questions and essay prompts in a way that made her application highly competitive. It also helped Krista refine her résumé so the judges know *exactly* what's she accomplished. If you want to know what you can do to make your essays and applications stand out, get *All the Wisdom and None of the Junk*. Here's the link:

http://boettcherfoundation.org/scholarship-book/

### Resource #7: Other People

## START A SCHOLARSHIP CLUB

A Scholarship Club is a super fun way to keep you and all your friends motivated during the scholarship application process. It's an excellent way to share ideas, support one another and celebrate each other's wins.

Don't worry about the competition among the group. There's enough money to go around. Our Secret Scholarship Club meets on a regular basis, and everyone's been able to take things to the next level because of their involvement in the group. You can take an inside look at what our Club does in the next chapter.

As you can see, there are a ton of resources out there to help you on your journey to winning thousands of dollars of scholarship money for college. Doesn't it feel good to know you have everything you need to start applying for scholarships?

# CHAPTER 11
## CELEBRATE YOUR WINS

## 📜 IT'S TIME TO PARTY!

You may think applying for scholarships is a long, tedious, drawn-out process that might not result in anything. If you feel this way, you're not alone. It can be easy to get discouraged. That's why it's important to celebrate the small wins along the way. Celebrating the initial steps you take towards achieving your goals will make you stronger, more capable and more confident.

**In our Secret Scholarship Club, we celebrate all the little things, whether that's finishing our résumés or applying for colleges. Here's our Agenda for the year. Notice how many times we celebrate...**

- *Discuss Scholarship Club objectives and agenda; Share Scholarship Hacking Secrets*
- *Write résumé; Use Résumé Template*
- *[Celebrate!]*
- *Learn Essay Writing Techniques and practice those Techniques*
- *[Celebrate!]*
- *Write general essay*
- *[Celebrate!]*
- *Set goals (individual and group)*

- *Set Rewards*
- *Make a Goal Meter to keep track of scholarships won*
- *Choose one of the three secrets to execute: start a business, start an organization, or do one big project*
- *Execute business, organization or big project*
- ***[Celebrate!]***
- *Go through Scholarship Search Secrets by Christopher Penn*
- *Execute any ideas from Scholarship Search Secrets*
- *Create personal Website*
- ***[Celebrate]***
- *Create business cards for scholarship applications*
- *Search for Scholarships*
- *Apply for Scholarships*
- ***[Celebrate!]***
- *Apply for Colleges*
- *Make t-shirts with our club logo*
- *Keep track of scholarships won*
- ***[Big party!]***

One thing people often do is wait for the big, huge win before allowing the small wins to be integrated into their identity. When you celebrate the small wins along the way, you feel like a winner. Giving yourself credit allows you to go on to the next step and keeps you motivated throughout the process.

**What are some things you can do to celebrate your wins?**

- Go out to eat
- Hang out with your friends
- Go shopping
- Buy yourself a gift
- Get a massage
- Tell someone about what you just did
- Journal about it
- Post it on Social Media
- Frame it

- Go on an outing
- Get a hug from someone
- Throw a party

**How do you integrate the small wins into your identity?**

1. **THINK:** Think about your accomplishments, the small steps you took, the connections you made, and the things that brought you joy
2. **FEEL:** Allow yourself to actually FEEL the excitement, satisfaction, and pride that comes from accomplishing a task
3. **SHARE:** Share the win *with enthusiasm* with someone

*Adapted from Brendon Burchard's Celebrate the Small Wins YouTube video. Brendon Burchard is a #1 New York Times Bestselling Author and one of the Top 100 Most Followed Public Figures on Facebook.*

One of the crazy things we do to celebrate our wins is this… we get in a circle and each person tells *with gusto* what he/she just did. Then everyone else goes CRAZY yelling and screaming, high-fiving and hugging that person, and telling them how awesome they are. That person's job is just to take it all in! Then, the next person gets his/her chance to share what he/she accomplished. We go around the circle until every person has had the opportunity to experience the love, excitement, and support from everyone else. It truly is an amazing experience to be celebrated in that way and to celebrate the wins of others.

## ⌐☞ BELIEVE IN YOURSELF

We've been very strategic over the years when it comes to preparing to win scholarships. My kids have spent their free time running for positions at school, going to leadership camps, and serving in the community. They could have worked traditional jobs, but the focus has been service and volunteering. So far, it has paid off. They have grown into caring and contributing members of society who are happy at the core because they are generous givers. Volunteering and serving others takes us outside of ourselves and helps us empathize with others. It shapes us into great human beings.

Even though applying for scholarships might feel like a shot in the dark at times, believe in yourself and in the process. Believe in your ability to figure things out. Keep writing those essays and submitting your applications. There are billions of dollars out there earmarked for YOU. Someone literally wants to give that money away.

It doesn't matter what your age is. It doesn't matter whether you're an *A* student or a *C* student. It doesn't matter what you've done or haven't done in the past. **What matters most is what you're choosing to do now.** The absolute best place you can start is with one of the top three scholarship hacking secrets...

- *CREATE YOUR OWN COMMUNITY SERVICE ORGANIZATION*
- *CREATE YOUR OWN BUSINESS*
- *BECOME A PROJECT MANAGER*

Doing one of these three things will give you the edge you need to win the scholarship money you need in order to go to the college of your dreams. Go for it with gusto and you may actually find yourself the grateful recipient of thousands of dollars of scholarship money! *Wouldn't that be awesome?*

Now that you know what the top three scholarship hacking secrets are, you are officially a Scholarship Hacker! *Congratulations!* Because of your desire to learn more about the scholarship application process and your willingness to do what it takes to be the best you can be, the following sums up who you are as a Scholarship Hacker...

# $ch🌐lar$hip *Hacker*
## More Intelligent. More Dedicated. More Ambitious.

*SCHOLARSHIP HACKERS ARE MORE INTELLIGENT, MORE DEDICATED, AND MORE AMBITIOUS.*

Scholarship Hackers have a strong desire to achieve great things... and they do!

Scholarship Hackers...

- *Define their future*
- *Follow their passion*
- *Create success*
- *Leave a legacy*

Scholarship Hackers are motivated because they believe.

*YOU ARE A SCHOLARSHIP HACKER!*

# CHAPTER 12
## FINAL THOUGHTS AND NEXT STEPS

## 📜 HOW TO FURTHER GUARANTEE MY SUCCESS

So now you have learned the top three scholarship hacking secrets. That officially makes you a *Scholarship Hacker!* Congratulations! When you choose one of the three strategies to implement, you will be in the top 1% of students who are Community Service Founders, Business Owners or Project Managers.

You may be thinking, "How else can I increase my chances of winning scholarship money?" If you think writing impressive essays is something the scholarship judges look for, you're right. The essay is the one thing that will really help the scholarship judges get to know you on a personal level. You won't just be a list of accomplishments. You will be a real, genuine person.

If you've struggled with writing essays in the past, you're not alone. Writing essays can be daunting. It's okay. You just need someone to show you how. Because I want you to be successful, I've put together a *Scholarship Success Kit*.

The *Scholarship Success Kit* is packed full of helpful information, fill-in-the-blank templates, and specific examples to follow. If you want to learn how to take your résumé, essays, and scholarship applications to the next level, get the *Scholarship Success Kit*. Whether you're a good writer or a bad writer, it will help you write résumés and essays that will capture the attention of the scholarship judges.

For more information about how you can further guarantee your success by presenting yourself well, go to the following link now:

http://www.scholarshipsuccesskit.com

*Here's to your success!*

### 

Thank you for reading my book. If it was of value to you, won't you please take a moment to leave me a review at your favorite retailer?

If you have any questions or concerns, please don't hesitate to contact me at my email address below. I wish you great success as you begin this important journey.

Thanks!

Jeannie Schulman
jeannie@scholarshiphacker.com
www.scholarshipsuccesskit.com
www.scholarshiphacker.com